"You mean—you know what the Second Precept is?" I asked.

"The Second Precept," Whey said, flipping a cheese omelet with the precision of Carl Wallenda, "is that 'All We Have to Look Forward to Is Doom.' Let's face it—this civilization is the product of millions of mistakes, and millions more are to come. We must embrace doom as part of our collective consciousness. There is no hope. Things will never change. We're screwed, buddy. And most of us know it. My personal theory is that if we didn't have to pee in the morning, most of us would never get out of bed."

———————

McCoy Hatfield is the latest pseudonym for Billy Frolick, who as Ronald Richard Roberts wrote *The Ditches of Edison County*, and as Horace Dump authored *Dumpisms*.

D0376732

THE
PHILISTINE
PROPHECY

———— *An Unauthorized Parody* ————

McCoy Hatfield

A DUTTON BOOK

PLUME
Published by the Penguin Group
Penguin Books USA Inc., 375 Hudson Street,
New York, New York 10014, U.S.A.
Penguin Books Ltd, 27 Wrights Lane,
London W8 5TZ, England
Penguin Books Australia Ltd, Ringwood,
Victoria, Australia
Penguin Books Canada Ltd, 10 Alcorn Avenue,
Toronto, Ontario, Canada M4V 3B2
Penguin Books (N.Z.) Ltd, 182-190 Wairau Road,
Auckland 10, New Zealand

Penguin Books Ltd, Registered Offices:
Harmondsworth, Middlesex, England

First published by Plume, an imprint of Dutton Signet,
a division of Penguin Books USA Inc.

First Printing, November, 1994
10 9 8 7 6 5 4 3 2 1

For
Charlotte South Carolina "Porkpie" Hatfield

———————

"Let's Go Mets!"
John 3:16

ACKNOWLEDGMENTS

Never having written a book before this one (and having read only three), I must thank several individuals for their assistance, guidance, and support: My agent, Susan "The Terminator" Cluck, and her assistant, Suzanne Gentle; my attorney, Roger Poodles; and my editor, Deiter Snoreland, whose ability to catch a mixed metaphor and kill it like an irritating housefly speaks volumes. Finally, I would like to acknowledge the de-motivational tapes of Robin Anthony, specifically his "Life's Too Long" series.

CONTENTS

THE PHILISTINE PROPHECY

When McCoy Hatfield first shared his incredible story with readers—a mind-bending mystery, conundrum, and riddle, with just a touch of Grisham for the aesthetically undemanding—they were confounded and delighted. They told their friends, who in turn told their friends, who went and told their friends. You know, like on that shampoo commercial.

Almost exclusively through word-of-mouth (and some mime), the whole country began hearing of this mystical, enchanting tale. Only weeks after its release, thousands of readers had been enticed by the prognostications and their uncanny effect on their lives. Hundreds of others reported hard evidence of the book's predictions. Five individuals developed cold sores, with no apparent link.

Now you, too, can experience the visionary lessons and startling clairvoyance of *The Philistine Prophecy*. A fable full of gripping suspense and relentless hyperbole, it starts with the report of a missing document. The American government tries to suppress; citizens are largely ignorant of the book's contents, however, as it is found during the O. J. Simpson murder trial. But the invaluable manuscript contains vital information: thirteen truths that people everywhere must embrace as we hurtle helplessly toward planetary destruction.

You will discover this ancient tome with a man whose odyssey spans the globe—from the rolling hills of Georgia, to the Florida Turnpike, down into the cavernous fairway bunkers at Inverrary. It will not take you long to comprehend the thirteen precepts of new spiritual destruction, and how they impact social relationships, foreign affairs—even the realignment of major league baseball. The Koran, the Bible, the Torah, *Field & Stream*, Merv Griffin's autobiography, *Curious George*, *The Collected Ziggy*, and the magic of David Copperfield have all influenced McCoy Hatfield's landmark work. Look at your life through his mystical filters, and you may wish you had never been born.

AUTHOR'S NOTE

For decades, we have been knocking upon the door of eternal enlightenment. Often, spiritually speaking, there has been no answer. At other times, a strange clawing sound could be heard from the other side. In many instances, the door had wet paint on it.

Perception and reality are often completely intertwined. Yet the success of comedian Gallagher baffles even the wisest of sages.

We are entering an era of clear uncertainty, sure unfocus, and temporary foreverness. When will rap music end as a cultural phenomenon? Is it safe to eat sushi? Never have so many people perceived the imperceptible and experienced the unknown.

No science or religion guides us as the future unfolds. We only know that with each passing day we seem to get closer to it. And a collective consciousness continues to develop, one that straddles boundaries of race, ethnicity, and gender, but does exclude those who wear beanies with propellors on them.

Friend, what you are about to read, hopefully, will contribute to this global misunderstanding. If the story engages you, moves you, or has any visceral impact whatsoever, I implore you to recommend that everyone you know buy this book.

Please do not share your personal copy, as the energy force field you have imbued upon it will undoubtedly be sullied. It is imperative that each person have his or her own copy, for this is the purest way in which the thoughts and ideas can be communicated to as many people as possible. Plus, I already spent my advance.

Enjoy the journey. And remember—if you believe, anything is possible. Except, of course, removing a barbecue sauce stain from a linen bedsheet.

Phi·lis·tine (fil′i-sten′)

n. **a.** A smug, ignorant person who is deficient in culture and aesthetics. **b.** One who lacks knowledge in a specific area. —*adj*. Boorish; barbarous.

THE
PHILISTINE
PROPHECY

A PITIFUL
MESS

Of all the diners in the world, she had to pick Clem's Burger Hut.

But that was Sheila for you—unpredictable and spontaneous. At least that's how I remembered her.

It had been twelve years, perhaps fourteen, maybe even a decade since I had laid eyes (let alone anything else) on Sheila. Driving to Clem's, I wondered how she had changed over the years.

Was she married and raising a family? Following a spiritual path and contributing to society? Was she continuing to evolve as both a person and a woman? And, most importantly, had she gotten really fat?

As I walked toward the back entrance of the Burger Hut, I noticed that the night was clear and the sky was starry. Nothing beats small-town Southern life, I thought. The only evening sounds were the usual

The Philistine Prophecy

chirping of crickets and Clem's son, Farley, retching into a Dumpster.

Sheila was on her fourth helping of beef ribs when I walked in—and I was *early* for our meeting. She could always pack the vittles away, that girl. But this was the first time I had ever seen a group of onlookers placing bets.

"Hey, Sheila," I called to her, shoving my way through the crowd.

"McCoy?" she giggled with glee, looking up from her plate. "I hardly recognized you with that barbecue sauce all over your face."

"Uh-uh," I said, correcting her. "The barbecue sauce is actually on your glasses."

As the locals settled up their wagers and dispersed, Sheila wiped off her eyeglasses. This afforded me the opportunity to see how the years had treated her. Her eyes were still sparkling and green, and there were still two of them, one on each side of her nose, under the eyebrows. And Sheila always could fill out a sweater; unfortunately, she now filled out a goodly portion of the restaurant as well.

"How have you been?" Sheila asked.

"Something is missing from my life," I said, skipping the small talk. "I'm looking for answers to a few very big questions. And I'm willing to do just about anything and go just about anywhere to find them."

"Better be careful," cautioned Sheila. "Cat Stevens went to sit on some mountain in Tibet twenty years ago. Now the record company doesn't even know where to send his royalties."

"So, why did you call me?" I asked, subtly easing my way toward an answer to at least one question. "Do I owe you any money?"

"No, no," she assured me. "I was driving through town and I thought I would stop and tell you an unbelievable story, one filled with intrigue, drama, suspense, and adventure."

"This isn't the one about the traveling salesman and the farmer's daughter, is it?" I asked suspiciously. "Because if I remember correctly, *I* was the one who told *you* that one."

Sheila wiped her mouth. "McCoy, get a grip. I noticed you still have a little trouble walking erect, but do you think I might be able to relate a few sentences without getting your arrogant claptrap back in my face?"

With that comment I began to recall why Sheila and I broke up. There were two main reasons: We were incompatible, and we didn't get along. And the fact is, we had chosen separate paths in life. She was a cutthroat corporate climber in the burgeoning interactive computer synagogue industry. I, conversely, was a ne'er-do-well free spirit with old money, New Age leanings, Chronic Fatigue Syndrome, and suicidal tendencies. I had enrolled in more twelve-step programs than an Arthur Murray stalker.

I ordered my dinner as Sheila eyed the dessert suggestions on the chalkboard behind the grill. "So here's what happened," she continued. "An ancient document's been found down in Florida."

I cocked my head. "An ancient document, you say?"

"That's right, brainiac," Sheila confirmed with just a touch of her trademark sarcasm. "You following the story so far, or do we need to bring in an interpreter?"

The added pounds certainly hadn't made Sheila any more tolerant. "Go on," I said as the waitress brought my meal.

"From what I've heard, this scroll is more fascinating than a year-end double issue of *People*. Apparently it contains answers to life's most baffling conundrums. The complete bowling scores of Johnny Petraglia, too. Oh, yeah, and thirteen precepts that point to inevitable planetary destruction."

"Wow," I exclaimed.

"Incredible, huh?"

"I forgot how big the pork chops here were. I may have to take some home."

"McCoy, are you listening to this?" Sheila asked. "I mean, this is pretty heavy stuff."

I had to admit, she had piqued my interest. Proof that we were all doomed? I did want to know more.

"Make Friends with Disappointment," Sheila intoned as she inhaled a piece of my stale garlic bread, then tried to wash it down with watered-down root beer. "It's the First Precept of the document—that the world is a pitiful mess, and its inhabitants are disappointed on a regular basis."

"Really?" I asked quizzically as I started to saw away on my overcooked chop, which smelled like it was made from an old saddle. "I don't know if I necessarily agree with that."

"Have you ever noticed," Sheila continued, "that you never have *more* money than you thought you had in your bank account—only less? That if you didn't call your friends, they would never call you? Or that the night you're actually in the mood to watch *Empty Nest*, it turns out to be a rerun of the *only other one you saw all season*?"

Looking at my former lover, I had to wonder if she had been bludgeoned recently with a large, blunt instrument. "Can I get some hot sauce, please?" I asked, flagging down the waitress. But the request for tabasco was just a cover. Deep down, I knew that Sheila was right. Life sucks.

She went on to explain how she had gotten wind of the document's existence on a business trip to Fort Lauderdale. Sheila was dispatched to the area to conduct meetings with prominent rabbis about the possibilities of digital sermons and CD-ROM congregations. Temples of the future, she called them. The rabbis, naturally, were concerned that after thousands of years of tradition, they might be out of their jobs.

One of the locals tipped her off that Morris Code, a rabbi she was scheduled to see, had stumbled upon the remarkable document while searching for his golf ball on a links course in Key Biscayne.

The discovery of the manuscript had softened the agony of a disastrous back nine for Rabbi Code. This included a two-stroke penalty for an unplayable lie on the fourteenth hole when his ball, incredibly, rolled into the mouth of a sleeping flamingo.

Rabbi Code apparently read part of the document, but then, unfortunately, misplaced it in his condo. Nonetheless, the following morning he addressed his congregation and outlined its broad strokes.

"The unfortunate truth," Sheila recounted, "is that we are hurtling toward Armageddon. The end is nearer than we think. And our current, slow de-evolution is going to seem like paradise compared to what we're in for.

"The members of the temple were stunned into silence. Following his lecture—I guess to lighten the atmosphere a bit—the rabbi pointed randomly at a woman in the congregation and asked her to join him onstage. Then he performed several card tricks."

"Were they any good?" I asked.

"It was pretty tough to see from where I was sitting," Sheila said. "But he looked like he knew what he was doing. I mean, it was nothing a pro couldn't pull off at a wine-and-cheese party. But then, how much of the Talmud do you think David Copperfield has committed to memory?"

"Good point."

Sheila and I shared a moment of deep, meditative silence. Then, suddenly, an attractive couple sat down in the booth across from us. We overheard them tell the waitress that they were at Clem's to celebrate their first wedding anniversary. They ordered a moderately priced California sparkling wine and, their hands intertwined, toasted one another and kissed tenderly on the lips.

Shaking her head sadly, Sheila whispered to me, "Disappointment—it's all around us. Inside, he must regret ever having met her. Odds are she complains about her job, brought screaming brats from her first marriage to the relationship, and is up to her ears in credit card debt.

"He, on the other hand, has the stench of a true loser, and saying 'I do' was probably the beginning of the end for her. Ten to one he's an obsessive–compulsive who uses women as doormats, smokes cheap cigars, and watches televised fishing."

"Sheila—I'm telling you this as a friend," I responded to her diatribe. "You might want to lay off the java a little."

Then I ruminated on my own romantic alliances of the past few years. Alexis believed that the only way our relationship could work was if I got a job, took responsibility for my actions, and stopped being abusive toward her. As for the twins, Cathy and Alison—they just weren't willing to share me.

Maybe Sheila was right. Maybe disappointment was simply a dominant aspect of life.

"Have you heard of Synchronicity?" Sheila asked me.

"Oh, I've got all The Police's albums," I answered. "But that's not the best one. *Ghost in the Machine* really kicks ass."

Sheila went on to explain that Synchronicity was actually a theory hatched by some dead shrink named Carl Jung. She said that it was cosmically significant that these two miserable newlyweds would plop themselves down next to us at the exact moment that she was discussing disappointment.

"Don't you see, McCoy?" Sheila exclaimed. "It's no mere coincidence. We're going to hell in a handbasket, and the universe confirms this on a regular basis."

It was then that I fully comprehended how she and I had drifted apart over the years. Sheila had grown intellectually as well as physically; she was the product of too much schooling and far too much cholesterol. I, on the other hand, was slender and firm of body. But in terms of gray matter I made Forrest Gump look like a three-time *Jeopardy* champion.

"Sheila," I announced, sliding the dinner bill her way, "I gotta go. Those pork chops are making me feel a little queasy."

THE PREVIOUS NOW, HERETOFORE KNOWN AS YESTERDAY

I returned to my four-bedroom cabin on fifty acres overlooking Crystal Lake in the Majestic Mountains, which I had inherited from my grandfather. The next morning I paddled my polished solid oak canoe to the middle of the gorgeous lake, and listened to the herons nesting, and the quiet gurgle of rock bass.

Mine was truly a miserable existence.

I kept thinking about Sheila's story. I wanted to know what the other twelve precepts were. But I knew nothing about rabbis. And absentminded rabbis losing ancient prophetic documents near the Florida swamps? Forget about it. There was no way I could find this paper oracle.

Yet somehow, even though Sheila had treated me like dirt at dinner, I knew that we had reconnected for a reason.

The Philistine Prophecy

After getting home from Clem's, I had a dream in which I was playing croquet with Robin Anthony in Arizona. Robin is a so-called Despairist and de-motivational leader who exploded on the self-help scene a few years ago with a series of seminars entitled "Life's Too Long." He is also a healer, a shaman, an F.O.B., a tournament-level Yahtzee player, and my personal guru.

It was Robin who, in the dream, suggested that I drive to Key Biscayne to find the document. He even gave me directions and toll money for the Florida Turnpike, which has put half the state in the poor-house.

"Look for the scroll, McCoy," Robin intoned in the dream as he bent over and hit a carom that knocked my ball into the Grand Canyon. "And good luck with your next play." Luckily a flying Alan Thicke swooped down and made the shot for me.

This dream contained two powerful messages. One was that my purpose in life—at least for the time being—was to make that journey to Key Biscayne. The other was that I had to lay off the grilled onions late at night if I wanted to get any quality sleep.

That morning—the morning after our dinner—Sheila called me to report what was, for her, further evidence that her suspicions were valid.

"Someone knows that I am after the manuscript," she whispered. "When I got back to my hotel, the room had been cleaned but there was no mint on the pillow."

No mint on the pillow. What could this mean?

The Previous Now, Heretofore Known as Yesterday

With anyone else, this might have been some kind of code, like the CIA has been known to employ—"Blue November," "Red Alert," "No mint on the pillow."

But with Sheila, the literal absence of a small but refreshing candy on her bedspread could actually send her fragile psyche into convulsions. (Don't ask me how I could stand her for the three months we dated—that's a bigger mystery than where the document was.)

I couldn't begin to fathom the cosmic overtones of the past two days. Here I was—unhappy, lonely, tortured, and bitter. Seemingly from out of nowhere, a woman I had prayed I would never hear from again contacts me. She claims to have a lead on the verification of my deepest fears.

But Florida? Did I really want to venture down to the admittedly inviting beaches of Florida? True, I was unemployed. True, Spring Break—and the attendant bikini-clad vixens and inexpensive hot dogs—was only days away. But Florida to me was an exotic, enchanted place I had only read about when I was growing up.

Ah, what the hell, I finally decided, throwing all of my possessions into my '73 VW Bug and gunning the engine. I was living in Georgia anyway.

Synchronicity? Good luck? Call it what you will—I was frankly tantalized by the chance to get a taste of the truth, even if I had to drive a few hundred miles to find it. I was prepared for an odyssey that could last anywhere from an afternoon to a lifetime.

When I hit Tallahassee I pulled into a diner called

The Philistine Prophecy

The Truck Stops Here. I was working on a plate of fried ham hocks and mashed potatoes when a man suddenly, and with great urgency, approached me.

"Are you finished, sir?" asked the busboy.

"Get away from me," I barked, opting to be alone with my thoughts.

A few minutes later, I overheard the diner's cook talking on the phone about an ancient document that he had heard was somewhere in the Florida swamps.

Nah, I thought. *Couldn't be the same one.*

But as the cook continued, I found myself eavesdropping. And when he got off the phone, I asked him about his conversation.

"I couldn't help but overhear you discussing an ancient document . . ." I hinted.

"Yeah . . . ?" countered the cook.

"This isn't, by any chance, the one found by the golf-playing rabbi in Key Biscayne who started reading it but got tired and misplaced the document in his condo—is it?"

From the cook's expression, I had apparently violated his privacy, and for a second I thought he might cold-cock me with his meat mallet. "Look, nosy," he muttered between gritted teeth, "if you must know, this is just my day job. I'm actually an esteemed professor of anthropology at a large university."

The cook, whose name was Whey Holsom, explained that on a recent trip to South Florida he had heard about the discovery of the document, but he knew nothing of the contents—with the exception of the first three Precepts.

The Previous Now, Heretofore Known as Yesterday

"You mean—you know what the Second Precept is?" I asked.

"The Second Precept," he said, flipping a cheese omelet with the precision of Carl Wallenda, "is that **All We Have to Look Forward to Is Doom.** Let's face it—this civilization is the product of millions of mistakes, and millions more are to come. We must embrace doom as part of our collective consciousness. There is no hope. Things will never change. We're screwed, buddy. And most of us know it. My personal theory is that if we didn't have to pee in the morning, most of us would never get out of bed.

"Think of those who organized religion thousands of years ago," Whey continued. "they basically divided all human behavior into good and evil."

He cited several examples. Temple-building: Good. Satanic worship: Evil. Generosity: Good. Greed: Evil. Pat Riley: Good. George Steinbrenner: Evil.

"So—do you think you understand the Second Precept?"

"Ugh." I shook my head, nausea rolling through me. "I'm not sure those ham hocks were fresh."

When I returned from the restroom, Whey handed me a sheet of paper on which he had written the address of the motel where he had stayed in Key Biscayne. There were also some X's and O's and a Smiley face, but I ignored them.

"Let's look for the document together," Whey said, perhaps a little *too* excited. "We'll live off the land and sleep under the stars. Before we go, we can stuff our pockets with my homemade shark jerky."

The Philistine Prophecy

The last comment didn't sit too well with me—especially given the effect his greasy ham hocks were having on my colon.

"The shark jerky's a deal-breaker," I insisted. I had a feeling Whey would be a more effective explorer than he was a cook. He would have had to be.

"I don't want to be presumptuous," Whey back-pedaled, perhaps a tad hurt. "I mean, we just met. And you're probably a busy fellow—do you have time to go on an adventure like this?"

I felt committed before I left, then waffled on the first leg of the drive. This time, after Whey asked me if I was available, I flipped through my Filofax. Haircut next Thursday. Small Claims Court in three weeks with that guy whose poodle ate clean through my garden hose.

But this was not a decision to be taken lightly. Vital information involving the future of the Earth was at stake—data what could change the course of millions of years in the lives of trillions of people.

"Sure," I shrugged. "Why not?"

WHEY GONE

A s you might have guessed, Whey was fired for yapping too much on the job, which was fine with him because he could live off unemployment while we searched for the document.

As I drove him down to Key Biscayne, he continued talking about the manuscript, enlightening me and opening my eyes. Finally he barked, "I can't keep opening your eyes—either pull over or let me drive. You're obviously too tired."

I didn't want to tell him that his droning on about the document was making it hard for me to remain conscious, let alone operate a vehicle badly in need of a new clutch.

"Please," I implored him, "let's talk about something besides the damned document. Haven't you ever heard of a subplot?"

But it was no use. Whey ran right through my

signal. Then, much to my surprise, the windbag started talking about something of substance. Apparently there was a coalition of individuals who were going out of their way to suppress the contents of the you-know-what.

"But who?" I asked, pulling the car into a 7-Eleven for a fill-up. "Who wouldn't want the dark, insufferable truth about the human condition to surface?"

"Think about it," Whey countered. "Could you imagine Barry Manilow's audience hearing that our planet is on a spiritual collision course? Or devotees of Mother Teresa? Or the fan club of Joe Lawrence of TV's *Blossom*?"

I stuck the gas nozzle into the tank, depressing the handle to start the flow of fuel. "Wait a second. You're telling me that Barry Manilow, Mother Teresa, and Joey Lawrence are behind the suppression of the document?"

"Not literally," Whey explained after we bought some refreshments and got back on the road. "But we have reason to suspect they might be part of the master plot. In fact, it's what the Third Precept is all about."

"Wait a minute," I said. "You know what the Third Precept is?"

"You betcha."

"Spill."

"It's that **Paranoia Makes Sense.**"

I felt a chill in my bones that had nothing to do with the Slurpee I was sucking down my throat.

"Wh-what do you mean by that? Do you think I have dandruff? Is that what you're getting at?"

"Relax, McCoy. What the precept means is that we all have a God-given right to be suspicious. Chances are that the guy you think is following you *is* following you. That if you're afraid your boss wants you fired, he or she *does*. And whatever you do, don't ever get comfortable with the thought that Chevy Chase has made his last movie."

"Ugh," I said, shivering. "That *is* scary."

After seventeen hours, we had only made it to Gainesville. And Whey had just about had it with the average Florida freeway speed of twelve miles per hour.

"There's something really tragic about the people down here," he opined. "It's not just the slow driving. It's the lime green polyester pants in 130-degree heat. It's the wool macramé Superfly hats on eighty-five-year-old women. It's the white shoes. It's the WHITE SHOES!!!"

Whey's face turned crimson; he clutched his chest. Obviously he was having some kind of seizure. It seemed serious, but it could have just been his cooking. I grabbed the steering wheel and drove to the nearest exit.

Luckily, we were on Hospital Row. I pulled into the parking lot of the first hospital, called St. Joseph's—named, of course, after the patron saint of aspirin for children. I asked for the emergency room.

Upstairs, Whey was hooked up to a respirator. His

vital signs were faltering; a blood test revealed that traces of bacon were present.

"Why, Whey?" I sadly asked my new, and possibly soon-to-be-dead, friend. "Why, Whey, why did this have to happen?"

He gasped for air, muttering what I knew would be his final words.

"Needed . . . to advance . . . plot."

MY FARRAH LADY

As Whey lay dying, I had decisions to make. Sure, we had become close on the roadtrip. But was I obligated to sit at his bedside and listen to him wheeze his last breath? I started speaking aloud to myself, as I often did during psychotic breaks.

"That document has given new meaning to my life. I need to continue my odyssey."

"Document? Did you say document?"

No, it wasn't one of my dissociative personalities answering me—it was a tall, full-figured nurse who seemed pretty interested in what I had to say.

His name was Spalding Johns, if his name tag was to be trusted. But with the fear-laden Third Precept hanging thickly in the air—not to mention some pretty nasty hospital disinfectant—I wasn't taking any chances.

"What's your name?" I asked the nurse.

"Spalding Johns," he answered, relieving me of my doubts. "Were you by any chance talking about that ancient document?"

This was too incredible to believe. It seemed like everyone I bumped into knew about the document. From the room across the hall, we heard an elderly woman snap out of a seven-month coma.

"The ancient document found by the rabbi from Key Biscayne?" she yelled before being medicated by her grandchildren, who had spent the past half-year memorizing her will.

"Spalding," I said, "I know we've only known each other for a little over a minute. But would you be interested in quitting your job and helping me look for the document?"

"Would I?" he exclaimed. "Does the Pope shit in the woods?"

Spalding needed to give St. Joseph's three hours' notice to formally resign. This afforded me the opportunity to wish Whey a speedy, healthy recovery, pray for his soul, and riffle through his belongings. I made off with $2.74, a skate key, half a box of raisins, and a mood ring.

Traveling with the low-key but ornery Spalding proved to be a completely different experience from listening to Whey's constant chatter. In fact, after a couple of hours I stared to wonder if Spalding had had his personality surgically removed.

Nonetheless, it gave me a chance to admire the sights as we traversed the Florida Turnpike.

This was spectacular, scenic country, brimming

with the bounties of the earth. On any given block one could see a Taco Bell, Wendy's, Burger King, Pizza Hut, Long John Silver, or Sizzler.

Beyond them loomed the splendor and majesty of the malls, teeming with crowds competing for discount underwear and garish lawn furniture. It's been said that you have to drive through America to really appreciate it. And within four hours we had driven through McDonald's, Kentucky Fried Chicken, and Del Taco. Spalding didn't talk much, but he sure liked his Happy Meals.

Down near Lake Panasoffkee, Spalding perked up at signs leading to Vincent's, a nursing home.

Since childhood he had loved the nursing homes of Florida, not just because he was a nurse, but because they evoked so much for him. The bitter attitudes of the employees and the unsightly surroundings specifically drew Spalding to Vincent's.

When we pulled into the parking lot I began to sense the attraction. This was an institution, a prison for those whose crime was simply growing old. "If you live here, you don't have much to live for" was Vincent's motto. No question about it—this was my kind of place. I felt like offing myself almost immediately.

"Listen, I'm having a little stomach problem," Spalding announced, stumbling out of the car. "I've got to find a restroom."

"Shouldn't be a problem in a *rest home!*" I winked, but he was already too far away to hear my little joke, limping off in a most peculiar fashion.

My companion's little problem gave me a chance to take in the vistas of Vincent's. The concrete walkways were cracked, virtually reduced to rubble in some areas. The outdoor picnic areas, where family members visited together, were filled with rickety, water-logged lounge chairs.

Waste disposal was obviously a low priority at Vincent's. Behind every building, Dumpsters brimmed with pungent garbage.

"Pretty spectacular, huh?" I heard someone say.

"Are you in the Dumpster? Are you stuck?" I asked, panicking.

"I'm right behind you, bozo," said the voice, and when I pivoted there was a picture of loveliness behind me.

Her name was Farrah Jacquer. I would describe her as slender and womanly. If she was either of those things, that is. Truth be told, she looked like a young Linda Hunt. But as they say at the Braille Institute, love is blind.

"Been here before?" Farrah asked, with a certain lilt in her voice that made me think she was wondering whether it was my first time there.

I cocked my head, which is never quite as exciting as it sounds. I had a feeling that she was checking me out like a library book.

"No, actually—"

"Do you know about the ancient document that was found in the swamps?"

This was just getting too wiggy. I had met four people over the course of two days, and they all knew more about the document than I did. I was starting to feel as uninformed as Dan Quayle doing the *TV Guide* crossword puzzle.

Farrah leaned against a heap of kitchen waste, arching her back so that her pert breasts saluted. And I'll tell you right now, pal, my eyes saluted right back.

"Hey, tiger," she purred, licking her lips, "how'd you like to know what the Fourth Precept is?"

"Would I ever!" I answered, barely able to contain my lust.

I sidled up and she moaned in my ear, all breathy-like.

"Meat Equals Sleep."

"Meat Equals Sleep?"

"You got it. Old people need less sleep—that's a proven fact. So how do you think we get those codgers to sack out every night?" She lowered her voice to a whisper. "We ply 'em with cold cuts."

I was astounded. "But—can you prove this?"

Farrah smiled a knowing smile. "Of course I can prove it. When I'm not trolling complete strangers behind buildings at condemned nursing homes, I'm a nutritionist at a university in the Northeast."

"Is it Northeastern University?" I queried.

"I guess you're not as stupid as you look," Farrah cooed, pulling me toward her. "But I'd sure be willing to be proven wrong."

Before we went any further, I had to know about the Fourth Precept. Meat Equals Sleep? Huh?

"It's simple. Throughout the twentieth century, mankind—especially Americans—has gradually been moving toward the unconditional endorsement of vegetarianism as the best dietary choice.

"But if you want to really get some Zs—and who doesn't in this violent, ugly, unforgiving world?— you've got to consume meat. It slows your system down to a crawl. It blocks your arteries. I don't just mean hamburgers, either. I'm talking steak here, big boy. Sausage, pastrami, roast beef, braunschweiger."

"How about a little pork?"

"Later," Farrah said, "let me finish. Frankfurters. Ham. Salami and baloney. Bacon—Lord, yes! Thick strips of fatty bacon!"

Farrah was obviously invigorated by sharing her findings. Her saliva sprayed everywhere.

I couldn't help but think about Whey, horizontal in a hospital bed up north, overdosed on nitrites. Did he know the Fourth Precept? Judging from his cooking and present condition, he sure did.

We walked, arm in arm, to a beautiful, secluded garden where birds chirped and, not too far ahead, a natural geyser gushed.

"Look at you two—what a handsome couple!" said the geyser.

I was overwhelmed. The scenery was lush, I was being seduced by one of the country's foremost nutritionists, and the revelations of the document were making my head spin. I felt that thousands of years of humankind's confusion were lifting. It was becoming increasingly clear to me that the planet was entering a new era of consciousness and spiritual evolution.

Plus, it looked like I was going to get laid.

My Farrah Lady

Just then, two goons marched up to Farrah and me. "Damn," she said. "I gotta take this meeting. Listen—it was great talking to you. Let's do lunch. Ciao!"

BEEN THERE,
DONE THAT,
BUT CAN'T REMEMBER
WHEN, WHERE, OR
WITH WHOM

Spalding and I slept at Vincent's. The next morning we gorged ourselves on heaping helpings of sausage links and corned-beef hash. (It was touch and go for Spalding, but he did manage to keep his breakfast down. Thanks for asking.)

A visiting professor, Hugh Jeego, joined us for the meal. Jeego had recently become the lucky recipient of a government grant to study energy. For several years he had charted the career of actress Heather Locklear, who was appearing on two prime-time television shows at once, *Dynasty* and *T. J. Hooker*. Jeego was the first with the courage to postulate that the quality of neither program suffered, despite Locklear's grueling schedule.

"Energy is a fascinating field," Jeego declared. "You've heard the story of the woman who, horrified at the sight of seeing her Oldsmobile roll backward onto her grandson, actually up lifts the tail end to dislodge the boy?"

We all shook our heads. None of us were familiar with that one.

Jeego sighed. "What about when you're jogging, and it's extremely hot out, and you've gone a mile or so? You're convinced you can't go that extra mile, but something called a second wind kicks in . . . ?"

Again, the group collectively shrugged. "I hate jogging," Spalding whined. "It's really boring."

"What is it with you people?" Jeego huffed. "Don't you have any interest at all in human potential? In the conversion of thought to energy to motion? In the work of pioneers of the field, like Da Vinci, who did some of the earliest aviation experiments with paper kites? Or Edison, who created electrically generated mechanisms that became today's CD player and film projector? Or the Bee Gees, who singlehandedly put The Hustle on the map? Get with it, folks!"

Those at the table put down their cutlery and looked blankly at one another. We certainly had something to consider. Specifically, how we could rid ourselves of this gasbag. It was pretty early for Jeego's theories and postulations, and Spalding was starting to get a little indigestion.

"Dr. Jeego," Spalding said, "do you think you could recommend an effective antacid?"

As all things must pass, so did my meal. Then it was time for Spalding and me to leave Vincent's.

"You're splitting at just the right moment," Farrah

told us in the parking lot. "There's something brewing here, and it ain't Miller Genuine Draft."

"What's going on?" I asked.

"It's those fucking do-gooders," Farrah explained. "The people trying to suppress the document. They've taken over the nursing home. They were blasting Carpenters music through the P.A. earlier."

That was all we needed to hear. Fifteen minutes later we were back on the Florida Turnpike, and Spalding turned the radio on. It happened to be an oldies station; after a song ended, the deejay came on.

"That was the Fifth Dimension," he said. "Speaking of 'fifth,' the Fifth Precept of that ancient manuscript found by the rabbi from Key Biscayne is, **We're All Victims.**"

"Change the station," I said.

"Wait a second!" Spalding exclaimed. "Did you hear that? It was the Fifth Precept!"

"I couldn't hear it," I said. "See, when I was a kid, Mr. Harrigan, my music teacher, used to twist my ears when I played the drums badly. Then, as I got older, people seemed to actually enjoy whispering around me so that I couldn't hear. A pattern developed whereby everyone would just take advantage of me for the rest of my life. They still do—they sell me inferior merchandise, involve me in risky investment ventures, and sue me over the most petty things."

We continued to drive in silence.

"So what did I miss? What was the Fifth Precept?" I asked Spalding.

"Never mind," he muttered, shaking his head.

Hours later, as I was deep in thought, Spalding fell asleep. This was a problem, as he was driving. Not wanting to hurt his feelings, I popped a paper bag in his face.

"Huh—wha—what was that?" he asked, startled.

"Oh, nothing," I said, thinking on my feet even though I was sitting down. "Just—um—the engine exploding or something . . ."

We stayed that night at a motel in Tampa called The Doctoris Inn. It was nice to finally sleep in a real bed, although the room had a slightly sinister atmosphere. Perhaps it was the words "Die Commie Rat Bastards" scrawled in blood across the ceiling.

I wanted to watch the in-room entertainment, which featured a choice of the films *Bombastic Pork*, *Black Beauties*, and a double bill set in a plant store: *Florist Hump* and *Little Shop of Hubba-Hubba*.

But Spalding had something on his mind, a rare enough achievement for me to sit up and take notice.

"McCoy, we need to plot our next stop on the route toward Key Biscayne," he said.

Just then an infomercial featuring my guru, Robin Anthony, came on the TV.

"Let's face it, people—Life's Too Long!" Anthony shouted to thunderous applause.

"Who is this moron?" asked Spalding. He looks like Lurch from *The Addams Family*."

"Shh—I want you to watch this," I told him.

"Since we are all doomed, we need to empower ourselves by making choices," Anthony continued.

"In any given situation, our decisions are what will bring us whatever droplets of happiness we might find in this ugly world. So take every opportunity to look at your alternatives, consider them intelligently, and choose wisely."

"So which direction should we head tomorrow?" asked Spalding, sliding the map in front of me.

"I don't give a damn," I yawned, flopping onto my bed for some quality sleep.

The next morning Spalding had a vision that we should head toward a town called Yoobrakit Yoobyit, where he heard there was a mystical forest he wanted to explore.

"They're not going to make us buy anything, are they?" I asked.

"What are you talking about?" Spalding responded.

"Well, a lot of the times you hear about these mystical forests," I explained, "and it's really just an excuse to make you sit through these ninety-minute lectures about beachfront condos. Then it turns out that they're not even near the beach. They really get you on the fine print, those criminals."

"Get in the car, you jerk," Spalding barked, although as with most things he said, there was an undercurrent of deep affection.

On the way to Yoobrakit Yoobyit, we stopped at a junkyard to look around for parts for my VW, which was losing original parts faster than Michael Jackson in the eighties.

I was stunned to notice that the proprietor bore an

uncanny resemblance to someone I once saw years earlier. The problem was, I couldn't tell where I had seen the other person, what he had been doing, or whether or not I even knew him. It was all quite perplexing.

"Are you ready to go?" snapped Spalding, who still hadn't had his morning coffee.

"Spalding," I said. "That guy at the cash register? He might remind me of someone I think I may have known at some point in my life."

"Really?"

"Yes. It's eerie. I mean, we may have had a past life together, been related to one another, or maybe even shared some incredible, history-changing adventure."

I knew that somehow this man had played an integral part in one of my lives. I had to confront him. Taking a deep breath, I walked up to the front of the junkyard, where the man sat in a recliner, listening to a minor league baseball game on a transistor radio.

"Excuse me?"

"Huh?" The man turned down the radio and squinted at me.

"You look really familiar," I said softly.

"Yeah, yeah," he answered bitterly. "I played Brian on TV's *Nanny and the Professor*. But I don't sign no autographs. So just find what you're lookin' for and be on your way, before I blow your nosy fucking head off."

The Philistine Prophecy

In a way, the experience with the junkyard guy was actually a positive one. I had finally found someone in the world who didn't know about the document.

DOWEN AND OUT

The car overheated around Sarasota. We pulled into a service station run by a French mechanic named Neal Dowen.

"You need a new radiator," Dowen said, without even lifting the hood.

"He's a crook," Spalding whispered to me. "And I get the distinct feeling that he doesn't know what he's doing. Have you looked in his garage? There isn't one calendar featuring a well-endowed girl in cutoffs dry-humping a rachet."

I trusted Dowen, however. In fact, I could swear he reminded me of someone I once knew . . . but I wasn't about to try that one again.

Since the radiator would take a day to be shipped, Dowen offered to let us stay with him at a nearby campground. Spalding and I lit a fire, then stamped out as many of our belongings as we could and watched Dowen light a proper one.

"It seems as though you two are looking for something," Dowen opined. "Would it by any chance be the ancient document?"

"So—you know about it, too," I huffed.

"Mechanics—that is just a hobby," said the Frenchman. "I am actually a renowned statesman and humanitarian. My concern is that this generation leave the world as conflict-free as possible, so that all future species can cohabitate in peace."

Dowen then got up and heaved a boulder at the cranium of a passing weasel, which he proceeded to behead, fillet, tie to a stick, and roast. He licked his lips as he continued to talk.

"Are you two aware that we can pick up each other's auras?" asked Dowen. "That we each radiate and resonate at certain pitches? Do you believe in energy fields?"

Spalding and I looked at each other and shrugged as Dowen flipped his weasel.

"How about wheat fields? Strawberry Fields? W. C. Fields? Sally Fields?"

"It's 'Field'," I corrected him.

"Really? I always thought it was 'Fields.' "

"Common mistake."

"Listen," Spalding said, rising and walking toward his tent. "I hate to be a party-pooper, but I've had people lecturing to me for the past three days. I have to get a little shuteye."

I was transfixed, though. "These energy fields—they're like psychic b.o., right?"

"What does it mean, 'b.o.'?" asked the Frenchman.

"Body odor," I explained, feeling like I was starting to really understand. "If we each resonate an aura, it's sort of like our own distinctive 'thought aromas'—"

"Exactly," said Dowen.

"—so, the same way each of us has our own individual stench when we perspire, so do we have unique formations of mental energies around our beings."

As I had hoped, Dowen offered me half of his charred weasel, which was looking mighty tasty.

The two of us continued to talk long into the night, feasting on the rodent meat. After a couple of hours we heard some odd sounds emanating from within Spalding's tent.

"Good evening, ladies and germs," said a gravelly, Semitic voice. "Hey, a funny thing happened to me on the way to the club. A man walked up to me and said he hadn't had a bite in weeks—so I bit him. . . . But all seriousness aside—I think my wife might be dead—the sex is the same, but the dishes haven't been done in weeks . . ."

"Uh-oh," said a concerned Dowen. "This is bad. This is very bad."

"What's going on?"

"Your friend is channeling."

I had heard about this phenomenon—the spiritual

transfer of a physically deceased entity through a living one. But *who* was Spalding channeling?

"It could be Leonard Barr, or perhaps Myron Cohen," Dowen said knowingly. "It happens a lot in this part of the country."

"But—Leonard Barr? Myron Cohen? Who are these guys? Philosophers? Historians? Inventors?"

"Comedians. Opening acts who went fifty, sixty years without ever changing their material. Many of them ended their careers here in Florida playing retirement communities."

From inside the tent, we heard more from the gravelly, Semitic voice.

"Hey, is this microphone on . . . ? I know you're out there, folks—I hear you breathing! I ever tell you about my honeymoon in Honololu? All night long, this is what I hear—'Lou-ow! Lou-ow!' Listen, folks, it doesn't get any better than this . . ."

"Is there anything we can do?" I asked Dowen.

He shook his head.

By daybreak the bone-chilling incident had passed, and Spalding was back to his old sullen, unfriendly self.

"So what the hell were you guys talking about until all hours of the morning?" he asked us.

Dowen seemed diligent about not hurting Spalding's feelings or letting him know that his channeled comedy routine was more or less hack material.

"Not much . . ." Dowen winked at me. "Besides, it was a little tough for us to hear each other— 'Henny'."

"What did you call me?" Spalding asked.

"Oh, nothing—let's just say you're lucky we didn't have any tomatoes with us."

"Let's kick it to the curb, homeboy," Spalding whispered to me a few moments later as we packed our gear. "I think our friend here is getting loopier than a Slinky. You read *In Cold Blood*, didn't you? These country boys can schiz out pretty easy."

So hit the road we did, but not before I asked Dowen one final question.

"Neal, can you tell us the Sixth Precept?"

"Sure. It's **Keep the Radiator Filled.**"

I found this fascinating. Obviously our car trouble was just a metaphor—and another opportunity to learn one of the thirteen insights.

"Keep the Radiator Filled," I ruminated. "I think I understand. It's like the world is an 'engine,' and we each need to contribute in order to keep the 'radiator' filled so that we don't 'overheat'—that is, to prevent fires, floods, earthquakes, and other 'natural disasters,' that are actually physical warnings, the universe crying out to us that we are in danger of psychic self-destruction. That's pretty much what the Sixth Precept means, isn't it?"

"No, actually," said Dowen. "It means that if you own an automobile or truck, it's just smart to keep the radiator filled. Especially places like Florida, where it's usually hotter than a motherfucker."

HARD TO STOMACH

With a new radiator and a fresh start, Spalding and I rolled on toward the energy center of Yoobrakit Yoobyit.

"You'll dig the vibe of this place," said Spalding in the à propos patois. "It makes Sedona look like Hooterville."

After a few hours on the road, we noticed an odd mountain formation—a series of ridges that formed a fist, and a thin peak resembling the middle finger sticking up.

"That must be it," I opined.

When we drove into where the fist was, we were surprised to find a small, wooded community. When Spalding hopped out of the car to find a loo, a woman approached me.

I recognized her—but once again, I was unsure from where.

38

"Wait—give me a second," I said.

"I'm—"

"No, don't tell me—"

"McCoy, it's me—Farrah."

"Did you do something different with your hair? Are you frosting your tips? Highlighting? Have you always had bangs?"

She shook her head. "God, you're thick. We just met three days ago!"

Farrah and I ate at a five-star restaurant that had been built in the mountain village, despite the fact that the population was only thirty-seven. There was an hour-and-a-half wait to get in, but she had some pull.

"So what's the deal on this little village in the middle of nowhere?" I asked as we shared an appetizer, grilled prawns with mango chutney.

"It's a cover," Farrah explained. "This is the home base for a group that studies the document and lives out its precepts."

My angel-hair pasta with tequila chicken arrived. "Tell me about the group," I implored her.

"It's run by a powerful man named Norbert Lemming," whispered Farrah as she started on her entrée, peppered skirt steak infused with fennel. "He's supposedly the world's foremost authority on the document. McCoy, how many precepts do you know?"

"I know that we're all disappointed and doomed," I began.

Farrah rolled her eyes. "The average schoolboy knows the first two."

"Paranoia makes sense. Thanks to you, I know that meat equals sleep. Speaking of which, how's your steak?"

"Don't change the subject," she teased. "Actually, it's a little chewy."

"Do you want to send it back?" I asked. "I mean, is it chewy like it's a bad piece of meat, or chewy like they overcooked it?"

Farrah leaned in toward me. "I don't think I've ever known a man to pay so much attention to a slab of beef, yet treat a woman like a lady." She brushed her lips against my cheek. All I could think was "Huhmuhna, huhmuhna."

"Back to the document, soldier," Farrah said, all throaty-like. "So far I'm only moderately impressed."

"We're all victims," I muttered, stroking her thigh underneath the table. "And remember—keep the radiator filled."

Farrah let out a sexy yelp that told me she liked her men educated when it came to ancient documents. "Listen," I suggested, "since your steak is dry and I finished eating a half an hour ago, what do you say we head back to your room and—"

"Farrah, can I have a moment with you?" asked a tall man who had suddenly appeared at our table.

"Sure."

I had absolutely no doubt in my mind who the man was as I watched him berate Farrah in the corner of the restaurant. It was either her father, who seemed to be just a tad possessive of his little girl, or her brother, who was tracking her social life like it was the stock market. Or the guy might have been an ex-boyfriend, jealous that she was out with another man.

When Farrah returned to the table, she seemed slightly shaken up.

"Who was that?" I asked.

"Who do you think? It was Norbert Lemming," moaned Farrah.

"Just as I thought," I bluffed. "Tell me, just what is his relationship with your group?"

"He is the all-seeing and all-knowing. He has the mind of a Macintosh Powerbook, and the body of a pro beach volleyball player."

I shook my head, not wanting to hear what she was telling me, yet at the same time strangely compelled.

"Lemming monitors everything we do, from the way we dress to where we shop for groceries. He forces us to give him eighty percent of our income every month, and prods our brains with electrodes every night when we sleep. And each morning we have to watch a videotape of the same episode of *Silver Spoons*, and recite the dialogue in unison."

"Farrah," I said, taking her hand. "It sounds a little bit like a cult."

"Don't start that cult shit with me, McCoy. This is my choice. Besides, if I left the compound Norbert would have me flogged with table tennis paddles."

I could barely finish my dessert—raspberry chocolate mousse with vanilla bean sauce. Though I was looking for the light, I had ventured into the heart of darkness. I realized then that the document and its contents, like virtually anything, could be used for blind power—not just the verification I seeked that the planet was headed for destruction.

"What did he tell you?" I queried Farrah.

"This search for the document is bringing about conflict between our people and the do-gooders—those who think the world is actually a nice place."

"Manilow? Joey Lawrence?"

She shook her head. "Now they think the heavy hitters may be involved. You know, the relentlessly upbeat people. Olivia Newton-John. Tony Orlando. Doris Day. Henderson."

"Florence?"

Farrah nodded. I shifted nervously in my seat.

"McCoy, do you realize what you've gotten yourself involved in? That there is a conspiracy to block the precepts by individuals who actually have positive feelings about life? Do you know that this manuscript is going to be tougher to find than a parking space in San Francisco?"

Just then, Farrah grabbed my arm. "McCoy," she announced, "let's run for it—quick!"

I looked around me as we scurried out of the restaurant like espionage agents. But I failed to see anyone on our trail.

"What was that all about?" I asked when we were a good two miles away.

"That was a disappointing meal," Farrah huffed,

all but out of breath. "I just wanted to duck out on the bill."

Farrah tossed her mousey mane. In the moonlight she looked like nothing if not a young Lillian Hellman. I gazed at this woman who had begun to invade my thoughts and my dreams. Brainwashed. Dull-witted. Irresponsible about restaurant tabs.

It had to be love.

When I got back to the room I shared my story with Spalding—how I had, in one amazing evening, connected with my soulmate while entering the bowels of true evil.

"Ugh—please don't say the word *bowels*," he groaned, lighting a match as he dragged himself out of the bathroom. "I'll tell you about true evil—I just spent the last three hours with one nasty stomach bug."

The poor guy. I knew there was nothing worse than traveling with chronic digestive problems.

"I've got something to tell you, though," Spalding confided. "Reading the back of a bottle of over-the-counter medicine, I stumbled onto the Seventh Precept."

I sat up straight, giving Spalding my full attention as he read it to me.

"Always Consult Your Physician Before Using Anti-Diarrhetics."

Sage advice, indeed.

CAVING IN

At dawn I was nudged awake by Spalding. "Let's blow this pop stand," he said.

We threw our gear into the VW, which was having muffler problems and, unfortunately, woke up the entire village.

Before we left, I made a request of my companion. "We can't leave without making one last stop."

"Oh, my stomach's okay," Spalding assured me. "That stuff really worked."

"Spalding," I asserted. "How about easing up on the self-absorption pedal a little bit? I meant that we have to get Farrah."

We drove through the mountain community as surreptitiously as possible in the wheezing, chugging heap. Miraculously, I saw Farrah leaving the compound store and called out to her.

"Psst—Farrah—hop in!" I called.

"I can't," she said, shaking her head. "I've got the cable guy coming today. He said to expect him sometime between six A.M. and nine P.M."

"But your mind is being controlled by a dangerous man," I insisted.

"So then quit it."

"Not *me*, numbskull," I said playfully. "I'm talking about Norbert Lemming. He can't be trusted."

"All right," Farrah relented, cramming herself into the back seat of the VW.

We started off, confident that The Man Upstairs would know the way toward Rabbi Code and the ancient document. (The Man Upstairs was a guy named Harold, whose room was upstairs from ours. He had a map of Southern Florida that was more up-to-date than ours.)

Not more than ten miles from the Lemming village, though, I began to get the feeling that something sinister was happening to us. Farrah was halfway through singing the score from *South Pacific* and horribly off-key, but that wasn't it.

"I think there's someone behind us," I told Spalding.

"She's a passenger," he gestured toward Farrah. "Don't you remember? You were the one who wanted to pick her up in the first place!"

"Not her, cretin," I corrected him. "Look in your rearview mirror. Do you see the fifteen-foot-high military Jeep coming at us ninety miles an hour?"

Spalding shook his head. "Uh-uh."

A small missile crashed through the VW's back window, narrowly missing Farrah.

"How about now?" I asked Spalding.

He pulled over and for several hours the three of us hid in the underbrush as a convoy of Lemming's vehicles—clearly in pursuit—passed by.

"What do you think?" I asked Farrah.

"I like that Miata," she said, pointing. "Sporty, but rugged. The silver one's really cool. Get it all tricked out? You're stylin', dude."

"I'm talking about our situation," I explained. "We're in serious danger here."

"Oh. Whatever."

I turned away, annoyed at the lack of support I was getting from my alleged partners. Farrah was incapable of having an independent thought after spending years in the control of Norbert Lemming. As for Spalding, all he could think about were two things: his last meal and his next one.

When I turned back, Farrah was gone.

"Spalding," I said, "where's Farrah?"

He shrugged. "Got me, Ace. Where was the last place you put her?"

"She was right here. She must have been abducted."

We made a run for it as machine gun fire grew closer. Somewhere along the cliffs and mountain ridges, I lost Spalding. Bullets sprayed around me. My underpants were riding up on me. It wasn't a pretty picture.

I ducked into a small hollow that was forged into a

hillside. Dying was all I had ever wanted out of life. Yet now that it seemed within my grasp, I was overtaken by a sense of self-preservation. My life wouldn't end until my mission—to find the document—ended.

Nonetheless, the concept of death fascinated me, and I began to project what the experience would be like. What level of pain would I have to endure? A Monkees reunion concert? Playing canasta with my grandfather and his hacking cough? The Ice Follies? *Later with Greg Kinnear?* The Miss Teen America Pageant?

I felt myself drift, floating over the Earth and all its manifestations, perceiving my life for perhaps the first time in its entirety, from my beginnings as a boy, living alone in the hills of Georgia, misguided and confused. I had evolved into manhood; now I lived alone in the hills of Georgia, aimless and malcontent.

Then I saw the other beings of the planet—the plants, the animals, and then those who fall into their own categories—Michael Jackson, Cher, Bruce Jenner.

It was an incredible vision. The entire story of mankind revealed itself to me like a Strip-o-Gram. Suddenly I had clarity and purpose. I had to stay alive. I had to find the document. In short, I was tripping my brains out.

I left the little cave and ventured out to look for Farrah and Spalding. Walking up a mountain road, I encountered a man of the cloth.

"Name's Bernie," he said. "What do you need? Alterations? Inseams? You name it. I been a tailor for fifty-seven years. Here, take my card."

"The only thing I need altered is my experience," I told him.

"That's gonna run you a little extra."

"Do you know a Rabbi Code?"

"You mean, like, Hebrew?" Bernie responded.

"No—that's his *name*—Rabbi Morris Code," I explained.

"Oh, yeah. The ancient document guy. I been doing his pants since—since—let's see, when was *Texaco Star Theater* first on the air—1947? Or was it '48? Oh, sure. He was quite a snappy dresser. You know, for a rabbi." .

Bernie reminisced for a good three or four hours before I got any useful information out of him. He suggested that I head up the mountain toward a mission, where he believed I could be shown the route toward Key Biscayne.

His directions were good, and by dusk I had reached the remote chapel, which was run by a priest named Father Away.

"How did you get here?" he asked me.

"I took my limo," I sighed, rolling my eyes. "How do you *think* I got here? I hoofed it, Pops." I loved being sarcastic to priests.

"Were you involved in the uprising back in Yoobrakit Yoobyit?"

"You betcha. Then I lost my best friend and this girl I was trying to score with, got shot at, was almost run over, walked for about a zillion miles, had this nutty death fantasy, and ended up here."

"Be serious with me, son."

"Scout's honor, padre. Swear to you-know-who."

I talked to him in more detail about my experiences. Then the priest suddenly said he had to leave.

"Father," I asked, needy and perplexed. "What could be more important than helping a needy, perplexed soul like me?"

"Uh," Father Away said as he walked off, "I have to go somewhere to meet with some people to talk about some things . . ."

The explanation seemed reasonable enough. Plus, I was exhausted.

I was fed by the missionaries. While I was eating, a young priest sat down next to me.

"Father Away told me you had a cosmic vision," said the priest. "Perhaps I can help. My name is Phil O'Steen."

"Did you say—"

The young priest put a finger to my lips and nodded his head.

"Tell me about your visions," he said.

"I felt like I was in control—"

"Continue . . ."

"That the world was opening up—"

"Right, opening up—"

"And I was climbing down into it—"

"Climbing down . . ."

"Father Phil—please cut it out!"

"Cut it out . . ."

The Philistine Prophecy

He was definitely the most annoying person I had ever met. Not only couldn't I tell my story, he was repeating everything I said. I found him smug, arrogant . . . Philistine.

I ran off and then realized that the young priest did not really exist. I had been looking at myself.

Feeding on shrubs and berries that night, I wondered where Farrah and Spalding might be.

And the Eighth Precept rang in my head like a church bell: **"We're Hopeless."**

WHAT A CROCK

P hil caught up with me in his truck and offered me a lift back to the highway. In the front seat, deep in conversation with Phil, was a woman named Jolene. An intense-looking man who introduced himself as Ruggaluh occupied the back seat.

"I understand you're looking for the manuscript," he said.

"Maybe." There was something really pretentious about this guy, and I was damned if I was going to give him any information. Maybe it was the loafers he was wearing—the kind with the little tassels.

"I know where your friends are," Ruggaluh said.

I wasn't falling for that one. No siree. Not for a second. "Oh? Which friends?"

He moved closer to me. Perhaps too close. Farrah and Spalding."

I looked the other way, out the window. *Could be*

any Spalding and Farrah, I thought. I'm no fool. The manuscript talked about coincidences being possible.

"Never heard of them."

Ruggalah shrugged and asked Phil to pull over at a fork in the mountain road. He and Jolene got out, and the truck continued down toward the highway.

"So," Phil asked me, "what were you and Ruggalah discussing?"

"Nothing much."

"Did he offer any information about Farrah and Spalding?"

I snorted. "He offered, but—"

"So?" Phil asked, "Where are they?"

"I—I—blew it," I confessed.

"You blew it?"

"I was really standoffish with Ruggalah. It might have been a mistake."

Phil turned the wheel hard and stopped the truck.

"Don't take this wrong," he said. "But you really are a schmuck. That guy could have helped you."

Maybe he was right. I was a schmuck. A Philistine. A loser.

"Tell me about your childhood," Phil said. "We can probably get to the root of your problems by looking at where they started. What was your relationship with your father like?"

"Well, I was his son."

"Okay. I guess that's a start." Phil scratched his head. "Was he hard on you?"

"Maybe a little," I opened up. "For example, he always said he wanted me to take over his company."

"That doesn't sound so bad," Phil said. "What line of work was he in?"

"Whenever I asked him, he said it was none of my business."

Phil got out of the truck and paced. "What about your mother?" he asked.

"As I recall, she was Dad's wife," I replied.

"Uh-huh . . ."

"She was an angry woman," I recalled. "She belittled me with nasty names. She never bought me new clothes and I often went to bed hungry. She beat me frequently."

"So she was abusive."

"Oh, I don't know. That's a pretty strong word."

"I'm getting a sense that there is great dysfunction in your past," Phil said.

"Hey, man—I'm not here to be judged."

"But it sounds like your father wasn't much of a father. And your mother was one mother of a mother. An übermother, you might say."

"An übermother?"

"Right. You were raised by a non-father and an übermother. No wonder you're troubled."

Phil went on to say that since my mother was intelligent and intimidating, she played the role of the interrogator in our family dynamic. My father was more internal, in an innocuous but not insignificant way. And my sister was inward, insensitive, yet, because she was underage, ultimately an innocent.

"So let me get this straight," I said, finally starting to understand his theory. "My mother was an intelligent, intimidating interrogator, my father was not insignificantly internally innocuous, and my sister was an inward, insensitive innocent."

"Right."

"Interesting."

"Was there inbreeding?" asked Phil.

"The information is inconclusive."

Phil furrowed his brow. "You're pushing down your past, McCoy," he said. "Do you know what they say about denial?"

"That it ain't just a river in Egypt?"

"No, that it's an unhealthy way of dealing with one's problems."

Because I was willing to listen to his New Age psychobabble, Phil drove me all the way down to Caloosahatchee. Spalding had once said that a cousin of his lived there, so I thought it was worth a shot.

At the first convenience store we could find, I asked the proprietor where I could find Spalding's mother.

"*No hablo inglés*," the man said.

At the second convenience store we could find, I asked the proprietor where I could find Spalding's mother.

"Oh, ya mean Lenore? She lives in that house right over there." He pointed across the street.

Think what you will about coincidences. This was one I was thrilled for.

I said goodbye to Phil and dashed over to the house. Ringing the bell, I paced nervously. A thin, homely woman answered the door. I prayed that she was Spalding's mother.

———

What a Crock

"Who the hell are you?" she asked.

"She was definitely Spalding's mother.

"Good evening," I stammered. "I'm a friend of Spalding's . . ."

"He's eating dinner. Come back later," she said, about to close the door.

I gave her my best smile. "Listen, we've been searching for this ancient document together, and—"

"Look. My casserole's getting cold. I don't have time to hear your whole life story, Butch."

"The name's McCoy."

"Like I care."

Lenore led me inside, where Spalding sat at the dinner table.

"Wipe your feet," Spalding greeted me. "My mother gets nutso about that kinda stuff."

I sat down, famished, ready to eat anything that was set in front of me.

"Listen," Spalding whispered. "We've got to get out of here."

"You mean to continue searching for the document?" I asked.

"I mean because my mother has made her infamous Poultry Casserole."

I squinted at the crock in the middle of the table. "Poultry casserole?" I said. "As opposed to chicken casserole?"

There was no time to continue the conversation. Before I knew what hit me, we had said goodbye to Lenore, grabbed our gear, and hopped into a '78 Oldsmobile that was sitting in the garage.

After we had been on the road for an hour or so, I asked Spalding what the deal was with his mother's cooking.

"That house," he said, a tear welling up, "is where all my stomach problems started."

"And what's the difference between 'chicken' and 'poultry'?" I asked.

" 'Chicken' is cooked."

"Wow," I said. "You're right."

"In fact," he said, "sometimes I think my mother was actually the reason the Ninth Precept was created."

"The Ninth Precept?" I shouted. "You mean you can tell me the Ninth Precept?"

Spalding gunned the engine, leaving rubber on the driveway.

"**Never Eat at a Place Called 'Mom's.'** Especially *my* mom's."

SEARCHING THE COSMOS

O ur next mission was to find Farrah. Spalding had a lead over in Fort Myers.

We were pleased to locate her at the home of her sister, Gigi, who insisted that we stay for dinner.

"Do you believe in the power of dreams?" she asked us as she served up a ghoulish goulash of veal and lox trimmings. "Dreams run my life. Believe it or not, I even get recipes from my dreams."

Tasting the meal, we had no trouble believing this. They sure didn't come from Julia Child. "Isn't there anyone in this state who can cook?" Spalding asked me in hushed tones.

Farrah encouraged her sister to share one of her dreams with us.

"My driver's license expires," Gigi began. "I run over to the Department of Motor Vehicles, during lunch hour on a Friday. The renewal process takes five minutes, during which the employees are cheerful and friendly.

"I go home and make myself a bag of microwave popcorn. Over twenty-five percent of the kernels pop. While I'm snacking I watch a new TV movie starring Robert Wagner. *He doesn't have a neckerchief on.* It's as though he actually knows that this is the nineties.

"During the movie I flip through my mail. Included is a check drawn to me, the result of an accounting error made by an employer from years ago. There is not one computerized announcement from a former talk show sidekick leading me to believe that I have just won a sweepstakes.

"When the movie ends my mother calls and doesn't make me feel bad about anything. My father jumps on the line and unconditionally supports me in any life choices I have made.

"I attend a professional soccer game that is exciting. In the seat next to me is Billy Crystal, who doesn't imitate an old Jewish man once or mention any of his current projects.

"When I get home, I lie down for a nap, and not one car alarm goes off."

We were transfixed by Gigi's dream.

"Then what happened?" I asked.

"Oh," she said, lighting a cigarette. "Then I woke up and I had to eat and go to work, like every day."

"What do you do?" asked Spalding. We were obviously in the presence of an actualized woman who was conscious about her thoughts and actions and their impact on life.

"Oh, I'm a lap dancer at a place downtown called The Hellhole," Gigi said. "Hey—it's a living."

Over dessert—ham-infused flan and cappuccino—Gigi asked us about our journey.

"The Tenth Precept," said Spalding, "is crucial to us continuing our quest. Yet we have come to a crossroads, and don't know which direction to turn."

"We don't even know where the crossroads is," Farrah snorted sarcastically.

"Are," I said.

"Huh?"

"Are," I corrected her again. " 'We don't know where the crossroads *are*.' There *are* two crossroads—otherwise, it's just one road."

"Oh," Farrah smirked, "thank you, Alex Trebek. You sure *are* an asshole."

Farrah certainly could be touchy. Even so, this constantly-being-called-derogatory-name thing was chewing away at my self-esteem like Sparky Anderson with a bag of Beech-Nut.

Gigi thought to herself. "The Tenth Precept . . . the Tenth Precept . . ."

"Do you know anything about it?" I asked.

"Any of you happen to see the April issue of *Cosmopolitan*?"

"No," I replied.

"No," said Farrah.

"Was it the Bonnie Franklin cover?" asked Spalding.

"Uh-uh—Kristy McNichol," Gigi said. "Give me a minute."

Gigi started going through a pile of newspapers and magazines, and finally came up with the issue of *Cosmo* in question.

"Let's see, now . . . where was that?" she said, thumbing through the pages. " 'Does Your Inner Child Wet the Bed?' . . . 'Suede Vests: Poised for a Comeback' . . . 'Take Our Attention-Deficit Syndrome Quiz—or at Least Part of It' . . . Ah, here it is—'The Tenth Precept.' "

"Wait a second—you mean to tell me that *Cosmopolitan* published the Tenth Precept?" asked Spalding.

"That's right. Ready?"

We nodded. Gigi smiled. "I can't say that I agree with it. But here goes. It says, **'Don't Look Forward.' "**

The group eyed each other, wondering who would be the first to address the Tenth Precept and its meaning.

Spalding broke the silence. Then he said, "Where's the john in this place?"

"Can you wait a minute?" asked Farrah.

"Barely."

"Well, this is important," she continued. "I *do* agree with the precept. Despite what my sister says, dreams are useless. I mean, how many people do you know who have actually lived out their dreams?"

"One," I said. "Have you ever seen the guy with no arms who plays the guitar with his feet?"

"I think so," said Spalding.

"All right," Farrah conceded. "Fair enough. But *aside* from the guy with no arms who plays the guitar with his feet. Most of us aren't dreaming—we're delusional. We walk around hoping that we'll hit the lottery, find jobs we like, grab the brass ring, and develop meaningful relationships. But what happens? Well, what we actually hit is each other. What we find is despair. What we grab are opportunities to be corrupt. And what we develop . . . uh, are our banal vacation photos—at the nearest drugstore."

"That last one was a bit of a stretch," I said.

"Hey, they can't all be gems," shrugged Gigi.

ISN'T THIS GETTING EXCITING?

On Everglades Parkway Farrah suggested a new strategy for finding the document.

"Let's send out positive energy."

"Let's not and say we did," countered the ever-positive Spalding.

"Hear me out."

"Hear you out? I'd like to *throw* you out," muttered Spalding. "Do me a favor, toots. Let me do the driving and Spaceboy over there do the thinking. You want to strategize? Grab a pillow and strategize a little shuteye."

As with virtually everything Spalding said, there was more than a trace of sarcasm in his voice. But I was willing to listen to Farrah's perspective.

"We're operating from a place of fear," she began. "We're scared that we don't know which direction to go. Scared of the food we're being served. Scared that the coalition to prevent the document from surfacing will thwart us."

"Hey, getting thwarted is *never* pretty," I observed.

"Really," Spalding giggled. "You never hear that somebody enjoyed a good thwarting."

"True," Farrah conceded. "But it's the imagery we carry in our heads that leads us to make poor choices."

"I don't know what you're carrying in your head, lady," Spalding chuckled as we pulled up to a tollbooth, "but I hope it's not contagious."

Farrah snapped out of her reverie long enough to smack Spalding on the back of the neck. "I thought you were the *driver*, Ace."

At the tollbooth, the collector asked for $1.25. We paid with a dollar bill and a quarter. But the collector shook his head.

"You can't get there from here," he said.

"What?" asked Spalding.

"You can't get to Key Biscayne this way."

I pulled out a map and reached past Spalding to show the collector our route.

"That's not what I mean," said this unlikely holy man. "What I mean is, you'll never find the document with all of this bickering and negativity. I could hear you people from half a mile away."

"That's what I've been trying to tell them," Farrah said, nodding her head. "Say—would you by any chance like to come with us?"

Spalding turned back and glared at her. "Hey, this isn't *The Wizard of Oz* here," he whispered. "This wage slave has a name tag that says CLYDE on it. Didn't your parents teach you any judgment? This clown has 'disgruntled' written all over his face."

Spalding again faced Clyde. "She's not quite right in the head," he explained. "Her mother, uh, played semi-pro rugby during her third trimester."

We continued driving, down through Weston to the Fort Lauderdale area, past the lovely community of Woodmont in Tamarac, down through Hialeah and Miami Beach. And, finally, we saw a sign that made our adrenaline rush.

"At last!" Farrah exclaimed.

" 'DONUTS'!" cried Spalding with glee.

"Not *that* sign," I said. "Look—WELCOME TO KEY BIS-CAYNE."

Farrah read the rest of the sign: "HOME OF THE ANCIENT DOCUMENT NO ONE CAN SEEM TO FIND."

We pulled up to the Chamber of Commerce, where a town official by the name of Flip Twigg helped us.

"We're looking for a rabbi named Code," I informed him.

Twigg looked like he was about to snap once he heard our plan. The blood drained from his face and he looked ashen.

"M-M-Morris Code?" he asked.

"Right."

Twigg shook his head. "Why don't you folks just go back to where you came from?" he suggested.

"Why don't you do your job and give us the information we need?" Spalding countered, as demanding as Rush Limbaugh on all-you-can-eat fried shrimp night at Howard Johnson's.

Twigg led us into a room at the back of the building and locked the door behind him.

"Code has gone mad," he said solemnly. "We've heard all sorts of reports. First, he steps down as rabbi of Beth Midhla Temple. Then he resigns as Grievance Committee chairperson at his condo. Now we've been hearing reports—he's off his low-fat diet, he's starting to use his air conditioning."

"In other words—" Farrah said through the lump in her throat.

Twigg nodded. "You got it. Code's cracked." He shrugged. "He's isolated himself. He's cancelled his Call Waiting service. You can try to get to him. The press has. The do-gooders certainly have. John Davidson has been particularly aggressive. But this guy's reclusiveness has made it impossible to get to the document. Let's put it this way—if D. B. Cooper and Howard Hughes were Code's friends, *they'd* tell him he needs to get out more.

"The fact is, Morris Code has transformed into something we mere humans may not recognize. A monster? Perhaps. A mystic? Maybe. A shaman? Could be. An evil genius? I don't know."

"Sounds like he's become a madman," Spalding theorized.

Farrah was shivering. "Yeah—a madman gone mad."

Twigg wished us luck and provided directions to

65

The Philistine Prophecy

Wilting Pansies, the retirement community in which Rabbi Morris Code had a condominium unit.

Security was minimal at the entrance. A minor altercation had erupted at a shuffleboard court, but otherwise it was business as usual, as one would imagine it to be. Mah-Jongg, gardening, walkers.

Building 11 loomed before us. We walked up the stairs to Unit 203.

"I'm scared, McCoy," Farrah said, squeezing my hand. I kept up a good front. But the fact was, I was scared, too.

Spalding rang the bell, and a few seconds later we heard the shuffling of feet. But the door didn't open.

"Who's that?" said a voice from inside.

The three of us looked at one another. I elected to speak.

"Rabbi Code?"

"That's my name, too."

"I know."

"Who's asking?"

"My name is Hatfield. McCoy Hatfield."

The door opened, slowly. Standing before us was the bald, five-foot-one-inch possessor of our holy grail.

"What kind of a name is this, McHatfield?" asked Code.

"McCoy—it's a southern name," I explained. "I am not 'of the faith,' as they say."

"Can I fix you something?" he asked. "Come in, take a load off your feet."

Awestruck by this turn of events, Farrah, Spalding,

and I made our way down the entrance hall toward Rabbi Code's kitchen. On the walls were framed photos—of relatives, I assumed—and a shot of Code golfing. No doubt the image was snapped on the very links where he found the document.

Spalding and I sat at the kitchen table as Code put a pot of soup on the stove. "I made this yesterday," he said, "and it heats up beautifully."

Behind him I saw Farrah, ostensibly using the restroom, but in actuality beginning the search.

"You hot?" Code asked. "I'll turn down the thermostat . . ."

"We're fine," I assured him.

"So. What can I do for you young people?" asked Code as he sat down and salted his soup.

"Rabbi Code. We understand you are familiar with a certain . . . ancient document?"

Code put his hand to his forehead as Spalding and I surveyed his face for a reaction. He nodded quietly, like Marlon Brando in *Apocalypse Now.*

"The Torah . . . the Torah . . ."

Behind him, Farrah gave us the "stretch" sign so often used on television talk shows. It was clear she felt confident that she would soon locate the document.

"Yes," I said. "You're obviously well-versed in the Jewish scriptures, rabbi. But we're talking about a manuscript we heard you found while playing golf . . ."

"I don't play golf, Ronald."

"Ronald? Who's Ronald?"

The Philistine Prophecy

The rabbi started pacing the floor. "Who's Ronald? You are! You think I don't know my own nephew? Not that you would bother to pick up the phone . . ."

Twigg was right. Code was starting to crack right before our eyes, and it was a spinetingling sight. Farrah nodded to us—that was our cue.

"Eat, eat—you're skin and bones," Code implored us.

But it was too late. We were gone.

In the car, Farrah skimmed through the document, down to the Eleventh Precept, as Spalding and I looked on curiously.

"Hit the Brakes," she said.

MAKING BOOK

Not only didn't Spalding know that "Hit the Brakes" was the Eleventh Precept, he didn't know there was an eighteen-wheeler behind us.

Spalding went flying through the front windshield and was killed immediately. Farrah hit her head pretty hard against the cover of the document.

Ironically, the truck had been carrying poultry.

"Well, at least we've got dinner," a woozy Farrah said.

Then she squinted and asked me, "Who the hell are you?"

With Farrah mentally challenged and Spalding about to feed the worms, I had a series of ethical decisions to make.

Luckily, I had landed in a huge beanbag chair and was unharmed. "Farrah," I called, crawling back to the car from the outdoor furniture store where I was thrown, "give me the document."

"What document?"

This was too good to be true. Not the part about Spalding being dead and Farrah suffering severe brain damage. No, the part that was too good to be true was this: The document was mine—all mine.

I slid the object of my quest from Farrah's lap and planted a wet one on her cheek. It was important that I fled the scene of the accident before the truck driver and the police got involved. But first I needed to see what the Twelfth Precept was.

And wouldn't you know it—it said, **"Take What You Can Get."**

I felt that leaving Farrah there was justifiable. I mean, here she was, dumbstruck and rather helpless, But if she had shared in whatever profits I would reap from the document—come on, it's doubtful that her quality of life would improve. She was, you know, out to lunch. The girl didn't even know who I was, let alone herself. Hey, you know something, pal? I don't need to answer to you or anybody else, for that matter. Get off your high horse, and mind your own goddamn business.

Anyway, I was out of Key Biscayne faster than Bill Clinton runs out of excuses. All I had to do was get the document back to Georgia. I had a plan.

I also had a problem. I had no money—for food, gas, and the exorbitant toll on the Florida Turnpike. "Take What You Can Get" rang through my head. So I did just that. The Oldsmobile had a pretty big trunk, and inside was some camping equipment, a bowling ball, a set of golf clubs, a case of Wheaties, and an eight-piece bedroom set. I took the stuff to a local pawnshop and got two hundred bucks for everything.

Putting the pedal to the metal, I made it back home in a day and a half.

WHUT EYE LURNED

W hen I got home, I realized that the adventure I had just gone on had changed my life.

I popped a beer and started reading the document. A ball game was on TV. Life was good.

What had I learned? That we're doomed, doomed to live lives of disappointment. That life really is too long. That you've got to keep the radiator filled. Hit the brakes. Watch those anti-diarrhetics. And that we're hopeless.

I called a guy whose brother had once known someone who wrote a book. He set me up with someone at a publishing company, and we had lunch.

The publisher seemed interested and wanted to read the manuscript. I thought about "Take What You Can Get." I realized I was going to need to make a copy of the document—I couldn't give him the original.

I took the document to a photocopy shop in town, but when I went to pick up my order later that day, the lady behind the counter shrugged. She said they had no recollection of me ever coming in, no record of my having left any document, and that if I didn't leave the store she would call the police. Then she called a Rottweiler and two security guards. I could take a hint.

My life over the ensuing few months was uneventful. I had a new take on my existence. There was something sad, though, about the fact that the document was gone and my friends were either comatose, dead, or mentally impaired. I was lonely. I read a lot.

And one day, in the bookstore, I noticed a new release called *The Philistine Prophecy*.

It was the document. That witch in the copy shop robbed me blind. The book was published at the grass-roots level, became tremendously popular, and was eventually republished by a major outfit.

Naturally, I was more than a little angry. But the document had taught me to be in touch with that anger. I didn't need to buy the book—I had lived it.

But there was one insight I hadn't gotten around to reading, so I took the book out of the rack and flipped to the end. And there it was, in all its glory—the Thirteenth Precept: **"People Will Buy Just About Anything."**